Welcome Little Star

a memory keeper of mindful moments

Written & Illustrated by Tamara Hackett

Sweet Clover Studios

Copyright © 2018 Tamara Hackett, Sweet Clover Studios

All rights reserved. No part of this publication my be reproduced

or transmitted in any form or by any means, electronic or mechanical

without permission.

Published by Sweet Clover Studios

Written & Illustrated by Tamara Hackett

ISBN : 978-0-9948875-9-7

For more by Sweet Clover Studios please visit:

www.tamarahackett.com or email questions to sweetcloverstudios@gmail.com

Dedicated to my Mom. Miss you.

Disclaimer: The author/illustrator disclaims liability for the use of the material in this book

Dear Readers,

My intention for creating this book was to support and encourage the connection between little ones and the ones who love them.

By capturing emotionally based thoughts, moments and observations, I believe it can provide insight, understanding and compassion for these precious moments in time.

As a parent, I know this is what I would want to communicate to my children and as a daughter, this is what I would have wanted to know.

I truly hope this serves you too.

      Love,

          Tamara

Beautiful babe,

name: _____

Welcome.

date: _____

First –

YOU ARE LOVED

Always.

Before our eyes met,

I knew in my heart...

When I hold you in my arms I feel...

My hope is that I can always provide...

My little one,

as I look at you right now,

I learn from you every day.

Here are some things you have taught me about...

LOVE:

TIME:

FAMILY:

SLEEP:

Dear my little one...

I cried today.

Simply because...

These days my love, our days feel...

You laughed today.

    Let me tell you about it.

I see how you show your love by...

These moments, moments like this:

- _____

- _____

- _____

I never want to forget

Today, I watched you play and it made me feel...

My heart grew today seeing you with...

Something I experienced today with you:

It took my breath away today, seeing you...

....

....

....

....

....

I commit to you my love.

I commit to noticing who you are,

what you like and what you don't.

Here is what I noticed lately...

-
-
-
-
-
-
-
-
-
-
-

My darling babe.

When I dream of your future,

You remind me, dear one that...

I know our connection, it feels like this...

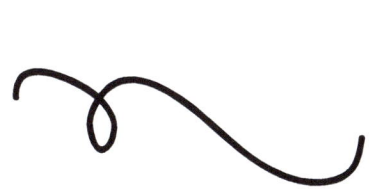

Every day with you is special.

Filled with a whole bunch of feelings –

happy, sad, excited, nervous, uncertain,

calm or not. Here are some feelings I felt...and why.

---

feeling:

why:

feeling:

why:

feeling:

why:

feeling:

why:

feeling:

why:

As you grow,

_____

_____

_____

_____

I can see myself in you when,

_____

_____

_____

_____

Being a new parent made me realize...

-
-
-
-
-
-
-
-
-
-
-

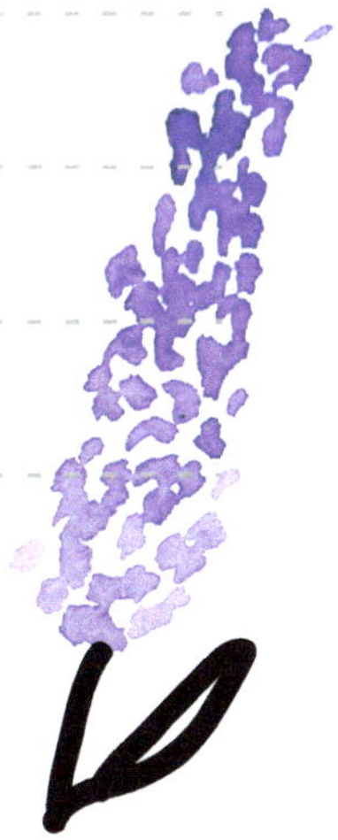

I hope you see the things that I see in you, my love.

Here are some beautiful qualities I've noticed in you so far...

Something I want you to know about me is...

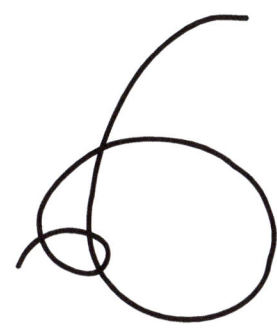

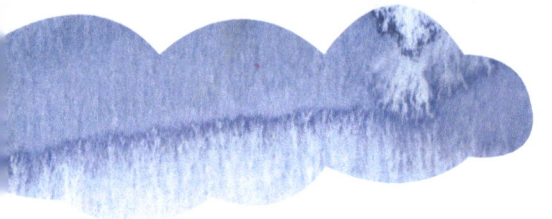

I wish for you...

....

....

....

....

....

Love always,

_____

date: